Copyright © 2023 Lynda Ruegg
All rights reserved
ISBN: 978-1-7380390-0-5

Joy Learns About God
How Big is God?

✝

Written & Illustrated by Lynda Ruegg

DEDICATED TO TURTLE
FAITH, TURTLE LOVE,
TURTLE STRENGTH &
TURTLE WISDOM

†

"Finally, brethren, whatsoever things are true, whatsoever things are honest, whatsoever things are just, whatsoever things are pure, whatsoever things are lovely, whatsoever things are of good report; if there be any virtue, and if there be any praise, think on these things."
Philippians 4:8 KJV

✝

Is God bigger than a tree?

Is God bigger than a tree, the mountains, and the sea?

Is God bigger than a tree, the mountains, the sea, and the sky?

Is God bigger than a tree, the mountains, the sea, the sky, the earth, and space?

God is BIGGER than a tree, the mountains, the sea, the sky, the earth, space, and YOU and ME!

God IS bigger than ANYTHING and EVERYTHING!

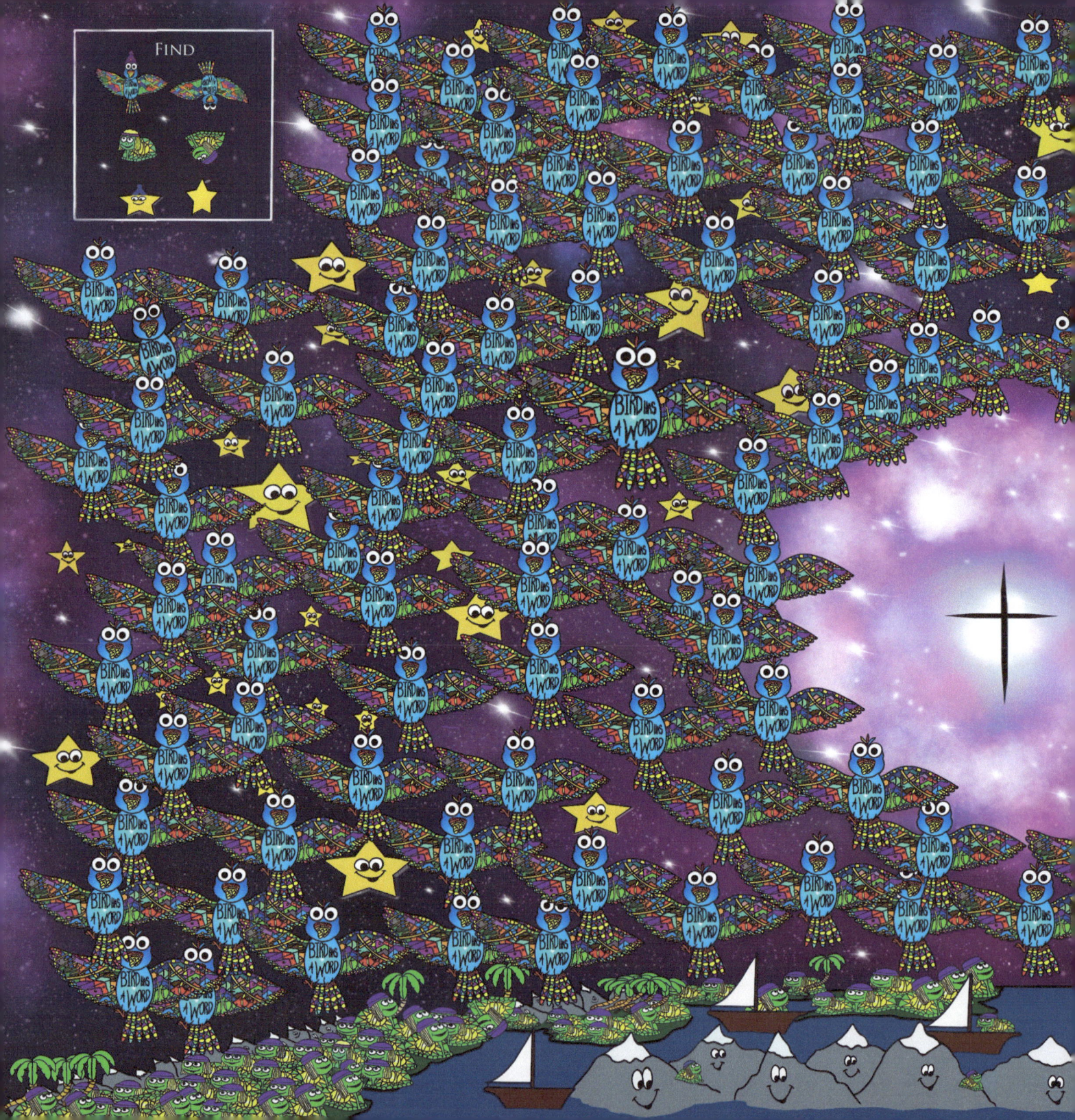

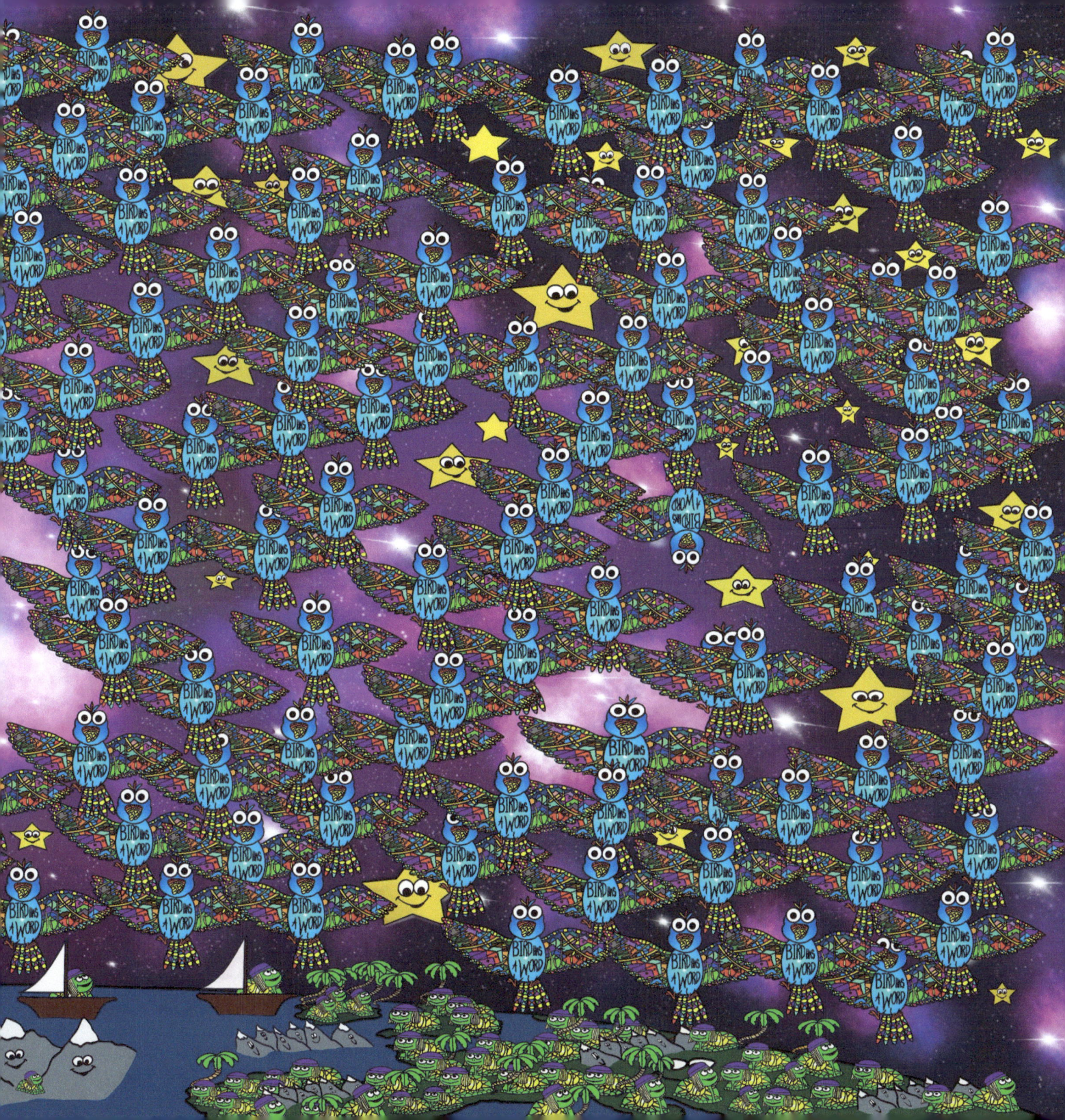